The Orange Storyhouse

OXFORD UNIVERSITY PRESS

Oxford University Press, Walton Street, Oxford OX2 6DP

Oxford   New York   Toronto
Delhi   Bombay   Calcutta   Madras   Karachi
Petaling Jaya   Singapore   Hong Kong   Tokyo
Nairobi   Dar es Salaam   Cape Town
Melbourne   Auckland

and associated companies in
Beirut   Berlin   Ibadan   Nicosia

Oxford is a trade mark of Oxford University Press

Titles in the Storyhouse series:

The Orange Storyhouse
The Yellow Storyhouse
The Red Storyhouse
The Blue Storyhouse
The Green Storyhouse

Three cassettes (twin-track) are available:

Orange Storytape

Storytape 1
for the Yellow and Red books

Storytape 2
for the Blue and Green books

Teacher's book New Edition

Printed in Hong Kong

Contents

Secrets

'She told me that you told her the
secret I told you not to tell her.'

'Oh, dear! I *told* her not to tell you
I told her!'

'Well, goodness, don't tell her that
I told you she told me!'

Me and the baby brother

First thing in the morning Dad said to me,
'Guess what? You have a baby brother
now.'

I said, 'I don't want a baby brother.'

He said, 'Well, you've already got him.
Isn't that great?'

I said, 'Where is he?'

Dad said, 'At the hospital—with your
mother.'

I said, 'Mum can come home and leave
him at the hospital. That'll be okay.'

Dad said, 'That's no way to talk.'

So I stopped talking.

After a while Dad said, 'We are going to
let you help name your baby brother. I
would like to name him Tom, and your
mother thinks Bill would be a good name.
What do you think?'

I thought. Then I said, 'Let's name him
Dustbin.'

Dad said, 'You are being very difficult.'

I said, 'Dustbin is a good name.
Nobody else will be named Dustbin.
Practically everybody is named Bill or
Tom. Dustbin. That's a good name for
him.'

Dad said, 'I think we'll do without your
help.'

I said, 'That's O.K. with me. I don't care what you name him anyway. Hey, how about that? You could call him Anyway.'

Dad said, 'He's part of our family now. I expect you'll get to like him.'

I didn't say anything.

7

Then my aunt came to take me to a
birthday party I got invited to before they
sprung the baby brother on me.

She said, 'Isn't it wonderful that you
have a baby brother?'

I said, 'Ugh!'

She smiled. 'Oh my, I'd like to be there
when he comes home. What will you do
when you first see him?'

'Hit him.'

Dad and Aunty looked at each other,
and then they looked at the ceiling. Aunty
said, 'You'd better get dressed, dear.'

So I got dressed to go to this yucky
birthday party. I used to like birthday
parties, but not any more. This one was
awful. First they all got mad at me when I
put mustard and salt and pepper on my
piece of birthday cake.

'Why are you doing *that*?' my aunt
asked loudly. She frowned.

I said, 'It's too sweet.'

Aunty said, 'Oh, I'm so sorry.' Only she
didn't say it to me, but to the yucky kid's
mother who made the gooey cake. Even
with mustard and salt and pepper it was
too sweet.

Then this kid pulled the cat's tail. So I
knocked him down and said, 'Be *gentle*!'
Why did they all get mad at that? You're
supposed to be gentle with animals.

Then I tried to take one of the presents
away from the yucky kid, and he yelled

like a baboon. I said, 'Share! Didn't anybody teach you you're supposed to share?'

They took the present away from me and gave it back to him. After the way they always tell me *I* have to share.

Aunty said I was spoiling the party and took me home. Boy, I didn't care one bit.

Dad came home early from work, and we made dinner together. We had chicken and rice and green beans, and for pudding he made chocolate sundaes.

I said, 'You're as good a cooker as Mum.'

He said, 'As good a cook, not cooker.'

Cook. Cooker. Who cares? I was trying to make a compliment. I don't think people should correct other people's compliments.

I said, 'You know what I'm going to be when I grow up?'

'What?'

'A bird.'

'A bird?'

'A bird without any children.'

He said, 'Why do you want to be a bird?' But he didn't ask why no children.

I said, 'So I can fly away.'

'From here?'

'Yes, from here.'

He said, 'You'd fly away from us, too?'

I said, 'I'd fly away so far, I'd fly away from *me*.'

'I see.' He sounded kind of sad.

'Well, I'd fly back. Probably.'

'That's a relief.'

After a while he said, 'Do you want to go to the hospital to see your mother?'

I said, 'Sure.' I waited for him to say something about the baby brother, but he didn't.

When we got to the hospital he said, 'If you want to wait in that room, I'll walk down the hall and look through the glass at—at the new baby.'

I said, 'I might as well come along.'

The nurse held up the baby brother for us to look at. Boy, is he *ugly*. I said, 'We'd better not call him Dustbin.'

Dad said, 'I'm glad you've changed your mind.'

I said, 'With looks like that, he needs a lot of help. Maybe you can call him Thomas William. Or William Thomas.'

Dad laughed. 'Maybe he'll get better looking in time.'

I said, 'I sure hope so.'

MARY STOLZ

Mart was my best friend

Mart was my best friend.
I thought he was great,
but one day he tried to do for me.

I had a hat—a woolly one
and I loved that hat.
It was warm and tight.
My mum had knitted it
and I wore it everywhere.

One day me and Mart were out
and we were standing at a bus-stop
and suddenly
he goes and grabs my hat
and chucked it over the wall.
He thought I was going to go in there
and get it out.
He thought he'd make me do that
because he knew I liked that hat so much
I wouldn't be able to stand
being without it.

He was right—
I could hardly bear it.
I was really scared I'd never get it back.

But I never let on.
I never showed it on my face.
I just waited.

13

'Aren't you going to get your hat?'
he says.
'Your hat's gone,' he says.
'Your hat's over the wall.'
I looked the other way.

But I could still feel on my head
how he had pulled it off.
'Your hat's over the wall,' he says.
I didn't say a thing.

Then the bus came round the corner
at the end of the road.

If I go home without my hat
I'm going to walk through the door
and mum's going to say,
'Where's your hat?'
and if I say,
'It's over the wall,'
she's going to say,
'What's it doing there?'
and I'm going to say,
'Mart chucked it over,'
and she's going to say,
'Why didn't you go for it?'
and what am I going to say then?
What am I going to say then?

14

The bus was coming up.
'Aren't you going over for your hat?
There won't be another bus for ages,'
Mart says.

The bus was coming closer.
'You've lost your hat now,'
Mart says.

The bus stopped.
I got on.
Mart got on.
The bus moved off.

'You've lost your hat,' Mart says.
'You've lost your hat,' Mart says.

Two stops ahead, was ours.
'Are you going indoors without it?'
Mart says.
I didn't say a thing.

The bus stopped.

Mart got up
and dashed downstairs.
He'd got off one stop early.
I got off when we got to our stop.

I went home
walked through the door
'Where's your hat?' Mum says.
'Over a wall,' I said.
'What's it doing there?' she says.
'Mart chucked it over there,' I said.
'But you haven't left it there,
have you?' she says.
'Yes,' I said.

'Well don't you ever come asking
me to make you
anything like that again.
You make me tired, you do.'

Later,
I was drinking some orange juice.
The front door-bell rang.
It was Mart.
He had the hat in his hand.
He handed it to me—and went.

I shut the front door—
put on the hat
and walked into the kitchen.
Mum looked up.
'You don't need to wear your hat
indoors do you?'
she said.
'I will for a bit,' I said.

And I did.

MICHAEL ROSEN

16

Nate the Great

My name is Nate the Great.
I am a detective. I work alone.
Let me tell you about my last case:
I had just eaten breakfast. It was a good
breakfast. Pancakes, juice, pancakes, milk
and pancakes. I like pancakes.
The telephone rang.
I hoped it was a call to look for lost
diamonds or pearls or a million pounds.
It was Annie. Annie lives down the street.
'I've lost a picture,' she said. 'Can you
help me to find it?'
'Of course,' I said. 'I have found lost
balloons, books, slippers, chickens. Even
a lost goldfish. Now I, Nate the Great,
will find a lost picture.'
'Oh, good,' said Annie. 'When can you
come over?'
'I will be over in five minutes,' I said.
'Stay right where you are. Don't touch
anything. DON'T MOVE!'
'My foot itches,' Annie said.
'Scratch it,' I said.
I put on my detective suit. I took my
notebook and pencil. I went to Annie's house.

Annie has brown hair and brown eyes
and she smiles a lot. I would like Annie if I
liked girls.

She was eating breakfast. Pancakes.

'I like pancakes,' I said.

It was a good breakfast.

'Tell me about your picture,' I said.

'I painted a picture of my dog, Fang,'
Annie said. 'I put it on my desk to dry.
Then it was gone. It happened yesterday.'

'You should have called me yesterday,'
I said, 'while the trail was hot. I hate
cool trails. Now, where would a picture go?'

'I don't know,' Annie said. 'That's why I
called you. Are you sure you're a detective?'

'Of course I'm sure. I will find the
picture of Fang,' I said. 'Tell me. Does
this house have any trapdoors or secret
passages?'

'No,' Annie said.

'No trapdoors or secret passages,' I said.
'This will be a very dull case. Now show
me your room.'

We went to Annie's room.
It was big.
It had yellow walls, a yellow bed, a yellow chair and a yellow desk. I, Nate the Great, was sure of one thing. Annie liked yellow.
I searched the room.
I looked on the desk and under the desk and in the desk.
No picture.
I looked on the bed and under the bed and in the bed.

No picture.

I looked in the wastepaper basket.

I found a picture of a dog.

'Is this it?' I asked.

'No,' Annie said. 'My picture of Fang is yellow.'

'I should have known,' I said. 'Now tell me. Who has seen your picture?'

'My friend Rosamond has seen it, and my brother Harry. And Fang. But Fang doesn't count. He's a dog.'

'Everybody and everything counts,' I said. 'Everything counts. Tell me about Fang. Is he a big dog?'

'Very big,' Annie said.

'Does he bite people?'

'No,' Annie said. 'Will this help the case?'

'No,' I said, 'but it might help me. Show me Fang.'

Annie took me out to the garden. Fang was there.

He was big, all right, and he had big teeth. He showed them to me. I showed him mine. He sniffed me. I sniffed him back. We were friends.

I watched Fang run. I watched him eat. I watched him bury a bone.

'Hmm,' I said. 'Watch Fang bury that bone. He buries very well. He could bury other things. Like a picture.'

'Why would he bury a picture?' Annie asked.

'Maybe he didn't like it,' I said.

'Maybe it wasn't a good picture of him.'
    'I never thought of that,' Annie said.
    'I, Nate the Great, think of everything.
Tell me. Does Fang ever leave this garden?'
    'Only on a lead,' Annie said.
    'I see,' I said. 'Then the only place he
could bury the picture is in the garden.
Come. We will dig in the garden.'
    Annie and I dug for two hours. We found
rocks, worms, bones and ants.
    But no picture.
    At last I stood up. I, Nate the Great,
had something to say.
    'I am hungry.'

'Would you like some more pancakes?'
Annie asked.

I could tell that Annie was a clever girl.
I hate to eat on a job, but I must keep up
my strength.

We sat in the kitchen.

Cold pancakes are almost as good as
hot pancakes.

'Now, on with the case,' I said.
'Where is your brother Harry?'

I met Annie's brother. He was small.
He was covered with red paint.

'Me paint,' he said. 'Me paint you.'

'Good,' I said. 'No one has ever painted
a picture of me, Nate the Great.'

Harry took his paintbrush. It was covered
with red paint. All at once I was covered
with red paint.

'He painted you,' Annie said. 'He painted
you.'

Then she laughed.

I, Nate the Great, did not laugh. I was
on a case. I had a job to do.

I looked around the room. Harry had
painted a clown, a house, a tree and a
monster with three heads.

He had also painted part of the wall, one
slipper and a doorknob.

'He does very good work,' I said.

'But where is my picture?' Annie asked.

'That is a good question,' I said. 'All I need is a good answer.'

Where was the picture of Fang?

I could not find it.

Fang did not have it. Harry did not have it. Or did he?

All at once I knew I had found the lost picture.

I said, 'I, Nate the Great, have found your picture.'

'You have?' Annie said. 'Where?'

'Look!' I said. 'Harry has a picture of a clown, a house, a tree and a monster with three heads.'

'Well?' Annie said.

'Look again,' I said. 'The picture of the clown is red. The picture of the house is red. The picture of the tree is red. But the picture of the monster is orange.'

'Well?' Annie said again. 'Orange is great for a monster.'

'But Harry paints with red,' I said. 'Everything is red but the monster. I, Nate the Great, will tell you why. Harry painted a red monster over the yellow picture of your dog. The yellow paint was still wet. It mixed with the red paint. Yellow and red make orange. That is why the monster is orange.'

Annie opened her mouth.
She did not say a word.
Then she closed her mouth.
I said, 'See! The monster has three heads.
Two of the heads were your dog's ears.
The third head was the tail. Yes, he *does* do
good work.'
Annie was very angry with her brother.
I was angry, too. I, Nate the Great,
had never been red before.
'The case is solved,' I said. 'I must go.'
'I don't know how to thank you,' Annie
said.
'I do,' I said. 'Are there any pancakes left?'
I hate to eat on a job, but the job was over.

We sat in Annie's kitchen. Annie and I.
And Harry.

Annie said, 'I will paint a new picture.
Will you come back to see it?'

'If Harry doesn't see it first,' I said.

Annie smiled. Harry smiled.

They even smiled at each other.

I smiled, too.

I, Nate the Great, like happy endings.

It was time to leave.

I said good-bye to Annie and Harry and
Fang. I started to walk home.

Rain had started to fall.

MARJORIE SHARMAT

Dinner
• Splodge •
• Stodge •
• Gristle •
• Scraps •

...Eat it all up — or Else!...

Bo Nancy and Tar Baby

One day, an old man who was once tricked by Bo Nancy decided to take revenge on him.

The old man built a tar baby and put it to stand up at a road junction where he knew Bo Nancy used to pass. In the right hand of the Tar Baby he stuck a piece of bread. Then he went home.

In a little while, Bo Nancy came whistling down the road. He saw the Tar Baby and thought that he would take away the piece of bread.

He went to the Tar Baby and said, 'Tar Baby, Tar Baby, give me piece of bread.'

But the Tar Baby did not answer.

Bo Nancy said 'If you do not give me a piece of bread I will hit you.'

But the Tar Baby did not answer.

Then Bo Nancy slapped the Tar Baby with his right hand and this hand got stuck. He shouted, 'Tar Baby, Tar Baby, give me piece of bread or I will hit you with my left hand.'

But the Tar Baby did not reply and Bo Nancy was so vexed that he slapped Tar Baby with his other hand. And this hand also stuck.

Bo Nancy said 'Tar Baby, I only asked

you for a piece of bread and you holding
my two hands. Why you holding me? Let
me go or I will kick you!'

But the Tar Baby said nothing.

Then Bo Nancy kicked Tar Baby and
his right foot got stuck. He said, 'Let me go,
I tell you. You really making me vex-vex.
Let me go or I will kick you again.'

The Tar Baby did not answer, and Bo
Nancy kicked him with his left leg and
this got stuck.

Now, Bo Nancy felt he should try a new
tack so he said 'Tar Baby, man you are my
friend. I was only making joke with you.
Let me go, man.'

But the Tar Baby could not let him go, so
he shouted, 'If you don't let me go I will
whip you with my tail.'

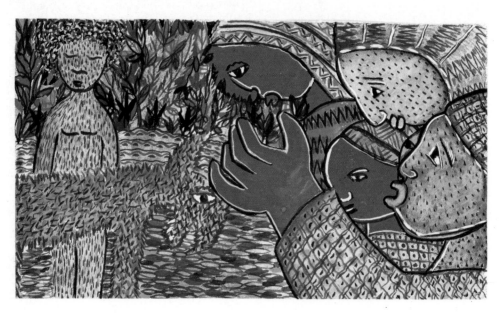

Tar Baby did not reply, so Bo Nancy whipped him with his tail and the tail got stuck.

Bo Nancy was very angry but he begged, 'Tar Baby, let me go, man. I like you man. I was only making joke with you. Why you holding me? Let me go, man!'

But Tar Baby could not answer, and Bo Nancy said 'Tar Baby, if you don't let me go I will butt you, you know.'

He butt the Tar Baby and his head got stuck. Now he was well caught.

By now, the old man was returning with his poui stick in his hand. He came up to Bo Nancy who begged, 'Old man, look how this scamp, Tar Baby, holding me and wouldn't let me go. I am your friend. Help me, man.'

The Old Man said, 'Yes, I will help you. Remember how you helped me when I was planting the yams in my garden?'

And the Old Man started to let him have the poui stick. He gave him blows like fire and Bo Nancy bawled and cried like a child until the tears helped to release his body from the Tar Baby and he crawled away.

By now, a crowd had gathered, and they all joined in laughing at Bo Nancy for he deserved what the old man had given him.

(Crick-crack, the wire bend, and so the nancy story end)

M. P. ALLADIN

The gingerbread boy

Once upon a time there was a little old man and a little old woman. They had no children but lived all alone in their little wooden house.

One day the little old woman made a little boy out of gingerbread. His nose was a currant, and two currants made his eyes. He had a row of currant buttons down his coat. The little old woman put the gingerbread boy in the oven to bake. Then she went on with her work.

When she came back into the kitchen, she heard a tiny voice calling, 'Let me out! Let me out!'

The moment she opened the oven door, out popped the little gingerbread boy and skipped across the kitchen floor. Away he went down the street, and after him ran the little old man and the little old woman. 'Stop, little gingerbread boy!' they cried.

But the little gingerbread boy said:

'Run, run, as fast as you can,
You can't catch me,
I'm the gingerbread man.'

Along the road he met a cow. 'Stop, gingerbread boy!' mooed the cow. 'I should like to eat you.'

But the gingerbread boy cried, 'I've run away from a little old man and a little old woman, and I can run away from you, I can.'

'Run, run, as fast as you can,
You can't catch me,
I'm the gingerbread man.'
And the cow could not catch him.

A horse came out of a gate on to the
road. 'Stop, gingerbread boy!' neighed the
horse. 'I should like to eat you.'

The gingerbread boy ran faster than
ever and cried, 'I have run away from
a little old man and a little old woman and
a cow. I can run away from you too, I can.'

'Run, run, as fast as you can,
You can't catch me,
I'm the gingerbread man.'
And the horse could not catch him.

'No one can catch me,' said the little gingerbread boy. 'I can run faster than anyone, I can.'

Soon after he met a sly old fox. 'Wait, little gingerbread boy,' said the fox. 'I should like to talk to you.'

But the little gingerbread boy cried, 'I have run away from a little old man and a little old woman and a cow and a horse. I can run away from you too, I can.'

'Run, run, as fast as you can,
You can't catch me,
I'm the gingerbread man.'

And he kept on running—but so did the fox. The little gingerbread boy ran faster—but so did the fox. Soon they came to a river.

The little gingerbread boy could not
swim, so he had to stop at last. The fox
caught up to him and said, 'Jump on my
tail and I will take you over the river.'

The gingerbread boy got on to the fox's
tail and the fox began to swim across the
river.

'You had better get on to my back,' said
the fox. 'The water is deep.'

The gingerbread boy got on to the fox's
back.

'You will get wet,' said the fox. 'You
had better get on to my nose.'

The gingerbread boy got on to the fox's
nose.

The fox reached the other side of the river and climbed out on to the bank. He tossed the gingerbread boy into the air and snap! he caught him in his mouth.

'Dear me,' said the little gingerbread boy, 'I'm a quarter gone.'

'Dear me,' said the little gingerbread boy, 'I'm half gone.'

'Dear me,' said the little gingerbread boy, 'I'm three-quarters gone.'

And that was all he said for he was *all* gone.

EILEEN COLWELL

How to make a man

Cut bark for the base.
Find moist soft clay.
Warm the clay in your hand.
Carve cleanly with your knife.

Shape the claw toes and feet.
Roll out the sausage legs.
Tree stump body. Branch arms.
Melon head.

Twist bark into hair like string.
Give your man a name,
The man with the curly hair.
Koo-kin-ber-rook.

Smooth upwards from the toes to the head,
Breathe into his mouth,
Blow air into his nose,
Shake blood into his heart.

Man stirs,
Man rises,
Man smiles with you
And speaks your name.

DAVID JACKSON

41

The journey

There was a mouse who wanted to visit his mother.

So he bought a car and started to drive to his mother's house.

He drove and drove and drove  until the car fell apart.

But at the side of the road there was a person 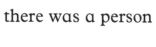 selling roller skates.

So the mouse bought two roller skates and put them on.

42

He rolled  and rolled

and rolled

until the wheels fell off.

But at the side of the road

there was a person

who was selling boots.

So the mouse bought

two boots 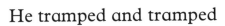 and put them on.

He tramped and tramped

and tramped

until there were

big holes in the boots.

But at the side of the road

there was a person

who was selling gym shoes.

So the mouse bought

two gym shoes.

He put them on and ran

and ran and ran

until the gym shoes

were worn out.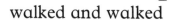

So he took the gym shoes off

and walked and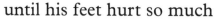

walked and walked

until his feet hurt so much

that he could not go on.

But at the side of the road

there was a person

who was selling feet.

So the mouse took off his old feet

and put on new ones.

He ran the rest of the way

to his mother's house.

When he got there

his mother was glad to see him.

She hugged him and

kissed him,

and she said, 'Hello, my son.

You are looking fine—

and what nice new feet

you have!'

ARNOLD LOBEL

The saucepan fish

'Now this is a funny thing,' said Monkey.

He stood beside the forest road, looking down at the strange round shining thing that lay quite still on the grass.

Man had just driven his rattly old car down the road, and this Thing had suddenly tumbled out of the luggage boot at the back. It made no sound as it fell on the grass, so Man did not know he had lost his new saucepan.

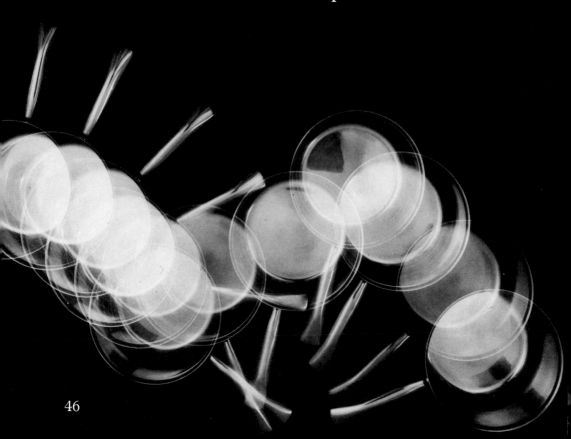

'I wonder if it's alive,' said Monkey. 'It doesn't have fur or feathers or hair, but it does seem to have a tail.'

He patted the saucepan gently and said: 'Hello, Thing. What's your name?'

After waiting to see if the saucepan would answer, he scratched his head and said to himself: 'I'll pull its tail and see if it squeaks.' He seized the saucepan handle and pulled. 'No, it doesn't squeak; it can't be alive. I'll see if Porcupine knows what it is.'

Porcupine was asleep in his burrow. He grunted crossly when Monkey awakened

'Of course it's not alive,' he said. 'It's a seat. Man sits on a seat, instead of on the ground as we do.'

Then he closed his eyes and slept again.

'A seat!' said Monkey. 'So that's what it is.' He turned the saucepan upside down, and sat on it; then he put a grass stalk in his mouth and made puffing noises.

'I'm Man, smoking a pipe,' he chuckled. It's a wonderful seat I have here, and I'm sure that Jay would like to see it.'

Jay was smoothing her bright feathers. She looked at the shiny saucepan and piped: 'It's not a seat at all, silly Monkey. That Thing is a mirror. Man looks in a mirror to see himself, instead of looking into the lake as we do.'

'A mirror!' said Monkey. 'So that's what it is.' He propped the saucepan against a tree trunk, and laughed to see his own brown face. Then he patted his head with his paws.

'I'm Man, brushing my hair,' he chuckled. 'It's a wonderful mirror I have, and I'm sure that Pig would like to see it.'

Pig was rooting. He looked at the shiny saucepan and grunted: 'It's not a mirror at all, silly Monkey. It's a hat. Man puts a hat on his head, instead of just wearing hair as we do.'

'A hat!' said Monkey. 'So that's what it is.'

He fitted the saucepan over his head, with the handle sticking out at the back. It was so big that it covered his face and rested on his shoulders.

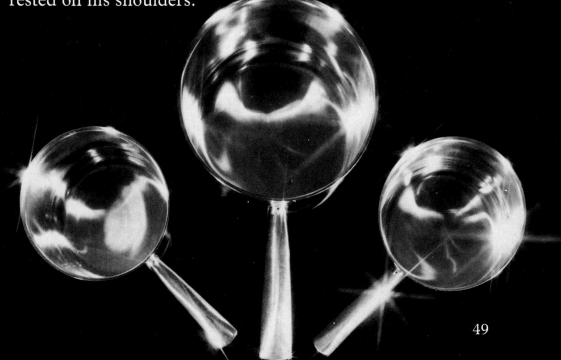

'Oh dear!' he grumbled. 'It's dark in here, and I can't see where I'm going.' He took the saucepan off his head, and knocked two holes in its side with a sharp stone. When he put the saucepan back on his head, his two bright eyes peered through the holes.

'That's better,' he chuckled, marching smartly along the path. 'I'm Man, going for a walk. It's a wonderful hat that I have, and I'm sure that Frog would like to see it.'

Frog was on the river bank, chasing gnats. When he saw the saucepan marching towards him, with Monkey's body and legs beneath it, he croaked in terror and hopped away.

'It's only me,' Monkey called him back. 'It's only me, and I've found a hat.'

Frog came closer. His eyes bulged as he stared at the saucepan hat. Then he said: 'It's not a hat at all, silly Monkey. It's a boat. Man floats on the river in it, instead of swimming as we do.'

'*I* can't swim,' Monkey told him.

'Then sit in the boat, as Man does,' said Frog.

Monkey sat in the saucepan boat, and Frog pushed it into the river. For a minute it floated. Then water poured in through the holes. With a splash and a gurgle it sank.

'Help!' yelled Monkey, thrashing his legs in the icy water. 'Help! Help! My boat has sunk!'

A big dark shape swam up beneath him. Hippopotamus appeared. 'Climb on my back,' he said. 'I'll carry you back to the bank.'

When Monkey was drying himself in the sunshine, he said: 'Thank you, Hippopotamus. Thank you for rescuing me when my boat sank.'

Hippopotamus looked at him kindly. 'You are really a silly little Monkey,' he said. 'That wasn't a boat at all.'

'What was it?' asked Monkey and Frog together.

'A fish, of course!' Hippopotamus smiled.

'A fish!' cried Monkey. 'What would Man want with a fish?'

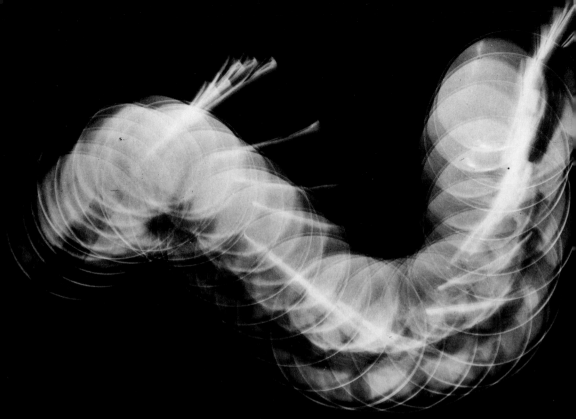

But Hippopotamus was back in the
river, blowing little popping bubbles, and
he would not answer.

'A fish!' said Monkey. 'Well, I can't see
it now, and that seems to mean that it
swam away.'

'It did have a tail,' said Frog. 'Yes,
indeed, it could be a fish.'

Frog and Monkey looked at each other
and nodded wisely.

'Hippopotamus is old,' said Frog.

'Hippopotamus is wise,' said Monkey.

'Hippopotamus is right,' they said
together. 'Of course it must have been
a fish.'

ANITA HEWETT

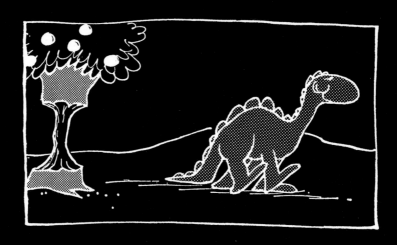

Supposing I changed into a rubber and every day more and more of me rubbed away...

The great sharp scissors

Once there was a boy called Tim who was
often naughty. Then his mother used to say
'*Tim!*' and his father shouted 'TIM!' But
his granny said, 'Tim's a good boy, really.'
Tim loved his granny very much. He went
to visit her often; and when he went, his
granny always gave him a present.

One day Tim's mother had a message
that his granny was ill. She decided to go
to her at once, and Tim said, 'I'll come
too.'

'No, you can't come,' said his mother.
'Granny's too ill.'

Tim scowled and stamped his foot. He
was very angry.

'You'll have to stay at home by yourself,'
said his mother. 'You'll have to be good. I
won't be long.'

Tim said nothing. He just scowled and
scowled.

'And if the front door bell rings, Tim,
you're not to let any stranger into the
house.' Then his mother hurried off.

Tim shut the front door, and then stood,
feeling angrier than he had ever felt before.
He listened to his mother's footsteps
hurrying away. When he could no longer
hear them, he heard other footsteps coming

from the other direction. They came louder, nearer. They came right up to the front door. There was a ring on the front door bell.

Tim just stood.

Then there was another ring; and then the flap of the letter-box moved. A voice—a strange man's voice—called through the letter-box: 'Tim, aren't you going to open the door?'

Tim decided what to do. He went to the door, and he put the chain on it, and then he opened the door, but the chain prevented its opening wide enough for anyone to get in. Tim peered through the gap of the door, and saw a strange man on the doorstep with a suitcase in his hand.

'I have things you might like to buy,'
said the stranger. He laid his suitcase
flat on the doorstep and opened it.

First of all Tim saw a notice inside, and
this is what it said:

WE
SELL
KNIVES
SCISSORS
BATTLE-AXES

'I'd like a battle-axe,' said Tim.

'We're out of battle-axes at the moment,'
said the stranger.

'Knives?' said Tim.

'Yes,' said the stranger. 'But what about
scissors? I have a most remarkable pair
of great sharp scissors.' He reached into
the suitcase and brought out an enormous
pair of scissors. The blades shone sharp
and dangerous. 'They'll cut anything,'
said the stranger. '*Anything*.'

'I'll have them,' said Tim.

'You must pay for them,' said the
stranger. 'Everyone must pay for what they
have, mustn't they?'

'Wait there,' said Tim. He ran and
fetched his money-box, and reached his
hand through the gap of the door and gave
the stranger all the money he had. In
return, the stranger gave Tim the pair of
great sharp scissors. Then he smiled at Tim
in a way Tim did not like, and went away.

Tim shut the front door and looked at the scissors in his hand. He clashed the blades together and remembered how angry he was. He decided to try the scissors out at once. The stranger had said they would cut anything. *Anything.*

He saw his father's coat hanging in the hall. With his scissors he cut off all the buttons of his father's coat. *Snip! Snap! Snip! Snap!* It was very easy.

Tim went into the living-room to find something more difficult for the great sharp scissors. He thought of the carpet. He cut the carpet in two—*Snip! Snap!* Just like that. Then he cut it again and again. He snipped and snapped at the carpet with his great sharp scissors until he had cut it into hundreds of little pieces.

Then Tim tried cutting the wooden leg off a chair. *Snip! Snap!* The great sharp scissors snipped the wooden leg off the chair just like that. Then Tim snipped the legs off all the chairs and off the table. He cut the sofa in two. *Snip! Snap!*

He tried the great sharp scissors on the clock on the mantelpiece. The blades went through the metal of the clock very easily indeed. *Snip! Snap!* and it was done.

He thought he would cut his goldfish in its goldfish bowl; but then he felt sorry for the goldfish. So he took it out and put it into the handbasin full of water. Then he cut the goldfish bowl with his great sharp scissors.

The blades went through the glass
without even splintering it. *Snip! Snap!*
Just like that. And the water from the
goldfish bowl went all over the floor.

By now Tim knew that his great sharp
scissors would cut anything. They would
cut through all the wooden doors and the
floors. They would cut through all the
bricks of all the walls, until nothing was
left. Nothing. Tim went and sat on the
bottom step of the stairs and cried.

Presently he heard footsteps outside.
They came up to the front door, and the
front door bell rang.

Tim was very frightened. He was afraid
the same strange man had come back. He
sat absolutely still, absolutely quiet.

Then a strange woman's voice called
through the letter-box: 'Tim, open the door
just a little!'

So Tim opened the door on the chain
again, and looked out. There was a strange
woman with a basket on her arm. She
smiled kindly at Tim. Tim saw a notice on
her basket. It said:

BUY
GLUES
INSTANT
INVISIBLE
UNBREAKABLE

Tim said: 'I've been using a pair of
great sharp scissors. I've made an awful,
awful mess of everything.' He cried again.

The woman said: 'Do you want to stick
everything together again with one of my
glues?'

'Yes,' said Tim. 'But I've no money. I used it all to buy the scissors.'

'Let me have those expensive scissors,' said the woman, and I'll let you have my best glue in exchange. You spray the glue round about and it sticks things together instantly, just as they were before.'

So Tim gave the woman the great sharp scissors, and she gave him the glue, and then she went off, and he shut the door.

Then he began to spray the glue, and it worked. He sprayed all the buttons back on to his father's coat. He sprayed all the pieces of the carpet together, so that it was whole again. He sprayed the legs back on to the chairs and table. He sprayed the sofa together again. He sprayed the clock together again, and the goldfish bowl—but, of course, the water was still on the floor. Tim put the goldfish back in its bowl, with fresh water. He'd just got everything straight again, when his mother came home.

His mother walked in, smiling.

She said: 'Granny's much better, and sends her love. I see you've been a good boy, Tim. Everything neat and tidy. I've a present from Granny, that she told me to take from her store-cupboard.' And Tim's mother took from her bag a pot of raspberry jam, which was Tim's favourite jam.

Tim said: 'The goldfish water is all over the floor.'

'Accidents will happen,' said his mother. 'I'll mop it up.' When she had done that, she made a pot of tea, and she and Tim had tea and bread and butter and raspberry jam. In the middle of it, Tim's father came home, and he had some of the raspberry jam too.

PHILIPPA PEARCE

Bear

There was a boy
who almost saw
a bear beside
his bed.

O bear, what are
you looking for?
He almost went
and said;

And are you looking
for a boy
that's fat, and nicely
fed?

But then he shut
his eyes, and thought
of other things
instead.

JEAN KENWARD

Nightmare

I never say his name aloud
and don't tell anybody
I always close all the drawers
and look behind the door before I go to bed
I cross my toes and count to eight
and turn the pillow over three times
Still he comes sometimes
one two three
like a shot
glaring at me with his eyes,
grating with his nails
and sneering his big sneer—
the Scratch Man

Oh-oh, now I said his name!
Mum, I can't sleep!

SIV WIDERBERG

The doko

In a small village in Nepal lived a man and his wife and their small boy. They were very poor and often they didn't have enough to eat. Moreover, the man's father lived with them. He had worked hard all his life, but now he was too old to work any more and he had no one else to look after him.

The old man needed a lot of looking after. His son and his daughter-in-law grumbled at him and neglected him, so the old man was thin and dirty. His clothes were worn out and he shivered all night on his mat in the corner where he tried to sleep. Most of the time he had only scraps of leftover food to eat. Sometimes the boy shared his food with his grandfather, but once his mother saw him.

'What do you think you're doing?' she asked sharply.

'Grandfather's hungry,' the boy answered.

'You leave grandfather alone,' said his mother. 'We've enough trouble as it is. And don't let me see you wasting good food again.'

The boy talked to his grandfather and helped him when he could do so without being found out, but things got worse. The old man coughed and complained. His son and daughter-in-law became more and

more short-tempered with him. They had
nothing to spare for him and he was in the
way.

One night when he should have been
asleep the boy heard his parents whispering
together.

'It would have to be a long way away,'
he heard his mother say. 'So far away he
couldn't come back.'

'Perhaps someone will feel sorry for him,'
his father said. 'If I leave him by the side
of the road someone might take him in and
feed him.'

'They *might*,' said his mother, 'but one
thing is certain. We can't put up with him
any longer. After all, we've got the boy to
think of.'

'I'll need something to carry him in. I'd better go to market tomorrow and get a good, strong doko.'

'Yes,' his wife said, 'and you can take him tomorrow night when there is no one about. We'll tell the neighbours that he wanted to spend his last days in peace and he's gone to live in a holy place.'

When the boy woke in the morning his father had already left for market.

'What are you going to do to grandfather?' he asked.

His mother was startled.

'Nothing,' she said. 'Why?'

'Yes you are,' said the boy. 'I know you are. You're going to throw him away.'

'That will do!' said his mother angrily. 'Whatever put an idea like that in your head? No. No, you see grandfather needs a lot of looking after. He needs someone to take care of him. So he's going to a holy place where he can spend his last days in peace.'

'Whereabouts?' the boy asked.

'Oh, a long way away. You wouldn't know if I told you.'

'Who's going to look after him?'

'Don't you bother about that,' said his mother. 'There will be someone to look after him all right. Now you keep out of my way. I'm very busy today.'

The boy's father didn't come home until late at night. He had a large, strong doko with him. After he had eaten he gave some food to the old man, then lifted him up and put him in the doko.

'What's this! What do you think you're doing?' cried the old man. 'Let me out!'

'Now, now!' his son said. 'You be quiet. It's all for your own good.'

'Where are you taking me? Let me out!' the old man cried again, shaking the side of the doko.

'It's all for your own good, I tell you. You know we can't look after you properly so we're taking you to a place where people can.'

'I don't believe you!' shouted the old man. 'You get me out of here.'

'Oh do please be quiet,' his daughter-in-law begged him. 'We're only doing what's best for you. You'll like it there.'

But the old man continued to shout.

'Liars! You want to get rid of me, that's what it is.'

He turned on his son.

'After all I've done for you,' he cried, 'and this is how you pay me back. You'll regret it, just you see if you don't!'

He shouted more and more.

The man ignored him. He set his lips tight and heaved the doko up on his back. The boy watched him as he opened the door to go.

'Father,' he said.

'What is it?' snapped his father.

'Father, when you've thrown grandfather away, please remember to bring the doko back.'

'Bring the doko back? What are you talking about?'

'The doko. Don't forget to bring it back because I'll need it when it's time to throw you away.'

His father stopped, turned round and came slowly back into the room. He put the doko down and started to lift the old man out.

SHYAM DAS BAISHNAB

Why the world stopped dancing

The world was very happy. Every night the
chief came to dance with them. And every
day they came to his house.

     The palm tree made his roof.

     The iroko gave him wood.

     The banana tree gave him fruit.

     The animals gave him meat.

     And the spiders and ants cleaned his
     house every morning.

The chief did not work at all.

     One day the chief said,

     'You give me a house.

     You give me wood.

     You give me food.

     Now I will give something to you.'

So the chief worked for many days.

     Then one night the chief gave his gift to
the world. It was a great drum. He played
the drum and the world danced. They
danced better than ever before. 'This is the
finest gift in the world,' they said.

     'Man plays for us. We dance.

     He plays for us. We dance.

     Let man always play for us, and we
     will always dance.'

     But after a time, the chief's family did
not come to dance any more. Only the chief
came. And one day, even the chief did not come.

73

The iroko was angry. He said,
   'Last year there were fifty men.
   Last month there were twenty men.
   Last week there were ten men.
   Last night there was only the chief.
   But tonight there is no one at all.'
The world was very angry. They said,
   'Let the chief play the drum.
   Let him play, and we will dance.
   This is what we mean.
   We will not dance without our chief.'
So they all went to the chief's house.
   The chief was giving a great dance.
'Why didn't you ask us to your dance?'
asked the world.
   But the chief said,
   'I am the chief of the world.
   I can do anything.
   I do not want to dance with the world.
   I want to dance alone.'
So the world went away. The trees said,
   'We gave him food.
   Now he is fat, and he will not play for us.
   Now we will stand in one place for ever.'
So the trees all stood in one place, and they
did not walk in the world any more.
   And the animals said,
   'We also gave him food.
   Now he is fat,
   and he will not play for us.
   Now we will hide from him for ever.'
So all the animals went away to hide.

The fish and the hippos went to hide
in the water.
The birds and the animals went to hide
in the trees.
And the spiders went to hide
in the grass.

The next day there was no food for the
fat chief. He looked at the forest, but
nothing moved. He called to the forest, but
nothing happened. And the chief was very
sorry indeed.

Soon the men went to the trees for their
food. They looked for animals for their
meat. The trees and the animals did not
come to them any more.

And that is why the world no longer
dances.

MARY BLOCKSMA

76

The knee-high man

Once upon a time there was a knee-high man. He was no taller than a person's knees. Because he was so short, he was very unhappy. He wanted to be big like everybody else.

One day he decided to ask the biggest animal he could find how he could get big. So he went to see Mr. Horse.

'Mr. Horse, how can I get big like you?'

Mr. Horse said, 'Well, eat a whole lot of corn. Then run around a lot. After a while you'll be as big as me.'

The knee-high man did just that. He ate so much corn that his stomach hurt. Then he ran and ran and ran until his legs hurt.

But he didn't get any bigger. So he
decided that Mr. Horse had told him
something wrong. He decided to go ask
Mr. Bull.

'Mr. Bull? How can I get big like you?'

Mr. Bull said, 'Eat a whole lot of grass.
Then bellow and bellow as loud as you can.
The first thing you know, you'll be as big
as me.'

So the knee-high man ate a whole field
of grass. That made his stomach hurt. He
bellowed and bellowed and bellowed all day
and all night. That made his throat hurt.
But he didn't get any bigger. So he decided
that Mr. Bull was all wrong too.

Now he didn't know anyone else to ask.

One night he heard Mr. Hoot Owl hooting and he remembered that Mr. Owl knew everything.

'Mr. Owl? How can I get big like Mr. Horse and Mr. Bull?'

'What do you want to be big for?' Mr. Hoot Owl asked.

'I want to be big so that when I get into a fight, I can whip everybody,' the knee-high man said.

Mr. Hoot Owl hooted. 'Anybody ever try to pick a fight with you?'

The knee-high man thought a minute. 'Well, now that you mention it, nobody ever did try to start a fight with me.'

Mr. Owl said, 'Well, you don't have any reason to fight. Therefore, you don't have any reason to be bigger than you are.'

'But, Mr. Owl,' the knee-high man said, I want to be big so I can see far into the distance.'

Mr. Hoot Owl hooted. 'If you climb a tall tree, you can see into the distance from the top.'

The knee-high man was quiet for a minute. 'Well, I hadn't thought of that.'

Mr. Hoot Owl hooted again. 'And that's what's wrong, Mr. Knee-High Man. You hadn't done any thinking at all. I'm smaller than you, and you don't see me worrying about being big. Mr. Knee-High Man, you wanted something that you didn't need.'

JULIUS LESTER

Why hares have long ears

Once upon a time a hare made friends with
a goat, and they started living together and
sharing everything.

One day the goat said to the hare:

'Let's build a house!'

'Let's!' answered the hare.

So off they went into the forest for some
logs. They came up to a tree and the goat
said:

'I'll knock this tree down!'

'You'll never!' said the hare.

'Oh, but I will. I'll just show you!'
answered the goat.

And he took a long run, and went crash! into the tree with his horns, and the tree fell down.

And the hare said to himself: 'So that's the way to knock trees down! Now I shall be able to do the same!'

And they came to another tree, and the hare said:

'I'll knock this tree down!'

'You'll never!' said the goat.

'Oh, but I will. I'll just show you!' answered the hare.

And he took a long run, and went crash! into the tree with his forehead!

And the tree still stood where it was before, but the hare's head had gone right into his shoulders.

The goat saw that he must get the hare's head out from his shoulders, and he caught hold of the hare by the ears and began to pull. He pulled and pulled, till at last the hare cried: 'Stop!'

But the goat still went on pulling. He pulled the hare's head back to its proper place, and his ears way out from his head!

And that's why hares have long ears.

VALÉRY CARRICK

Supposing one day I jumped as high as I could and didn't come back down again......

COWARDY COWBOY

A list

One morning Toad sat in bed.
'I have many things to do,' he said.
'I will write them all down on a list
so that I can remember them.'
Toad wrote on a piece of paper:

A list of things to do today

Then he wrote:

Wake up

'I have done that,' said Toad,
and he crossed it out:

W̶a̶k̶e̶ ̶u̶p̶

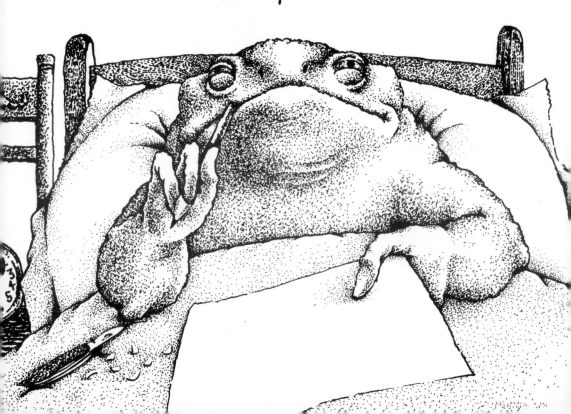

Then Toad wrote other things on the
paper.

A list of things to do today

~~Wake up~~

Eat breakfast
Wash up
Go to Frog's house
Go for a walk with Frog

Eat lunch

Take nap

Play games with Frog

Eat supper

Go to sleep

'There,' said Toad.
'Now my day is all written down.'
He got out of bed and had something to
eat.
Then Toad crossed out:
~~Eat breakfast~~
Toad washed the breakfast dishes and
put them away.
Then he crossed out:
~~Wash up~~

Toad put the list away. He opened the door
and walked out into the morning. Soon
Toad was at Frog's front door. He took out
the list and crossed out:

~~Go to Frog's house~~

Toad knocked at the door.

'Hello,' said Frog.

'Look at my list of things to do,' said Toad.

'Oh,' said Frog, 'that is very nice.'

Toad said, 'My list tells me that we will
go for a walk.'

'All right,' said Frog, 'I am ready.'

Frog and Toad went on a long walk.
Then Toad took out his list
again.

He crossed out:

~~Go for a walk with Frog~~

Just then there was a strong wind. It blew
the list out of Toad's hand. The list blew
high up into the air.

'Help!' cried Toad. 'My list is blowing
away. What will I do without my list?'

'Hurry!' said Frog. 'We will run and
catch it.'

'No!' shouted Toad. 'I cannot do that.'

'Why not?' asked Frog.

'Because,' wailed Toad, 'running after my
list is not one of the things that I wrote
on my list of things to do!'

Frog ran after the list.

He ran over hills and swamps, but the list
blew on and on.

At last Frog came back to Toad.

'I am sorry,' gasped Frog, 'but I could not catch your list.'

'Blah,' said Toad. 'I cannot remember any of the things that were on my list of things to do. I will just have to sit here and do nothing.'

Toad sat and did nothing.

Frog sat with him.

After a long time Frog said, 'Toad, it is getting dark. We should be going to sleep now.'

'Go to sleep!' shouted Toad. 'That was the last thing on my list!'

Toad wrote on the ground with a stick:

Then he crossed out:

'There,' said Toad. 'Now my day is all
crossed out!'

'I am glad,' said Frog.

Then Frog and Toad went to sleep.

ARNOLD LOBEL

Would you rather live with . . .

a fish in a bowl

a gerbil in a cage

a parrot on a perch

or a rabbit in a hutch?

Illustrations

Cover by Sarah Garland

Acknowledgements

The Editors gratefully acknowledge permission to reproduce extracts from the following copyright works:

JANET and ALLAN AHLBERG: 'Cowardy Cowboy' from *The Old Joke Book* (Kestrel Books, 1976). Copyright © 1976 by Janet and Allan Ahlberg. Reprinted by permission of Penguin Books Ltd. M.P. ALLADIN: 'Bo Nancy and Tar Baby' from *Folk Tales and Legends of Trinidad*. Reprinted by permission of the author.   JOHN BURNINGHAM: 'Would you rather live with . . .' from *Would you Rather*, illustrated by the author, Reprinted by permission of the author and of Jonathan Cape Ltd. MARY BLOCKSMA: 'Why the world stopped dancing' from *How the Earth was Satisfied* (1971). Reprinted by permission of Oxford University Press, Nigeria Branch.   VALERY CARRICK: 'Why Hares have Long Ears' from *Picture Folk Tales*. Slightly adapted and reprinted by permission of Basil Blackwell & Mott Ltd.   WILLIAM COLE and TOMI UNGERER: 'Secrets' from *Rhyme Giggles, Nonsense Giggles* (The Bodley Head Ltd.). Reprinted by permission of Laurence Pollinger Ltd. on behalf of The World Publishing Company.   EILEEN COLWELL: 'The gingerbread boy' from *Tell Me a Story* (Puffin Books, 1962) is a traditional tale and is now out of copyright.   JOHNNY HART: 'Oh, boy, an apple tree' from *What's New, B.C.?* © Field Newspaper Syndicate 1978. Reprinted by permission of Syndication International Ltd.   ANITA HEWETT: 'The saucepan fish' from *The Anita Hewett Animal Story Book* published by the Bodley Head. Reprinted by permission of the publishers. DAVID JACKSON: 'How to make a man' is first published in this anthology. Copyright © 1979 by David Jackson.   JEAN KENWARD: 'Bear' from *Old Mister Hotpotch* (Thornhill Press). Reprinted by permission of the author.   JULIUS LESTER: 'The knee-high man' from *The Knee-high Man and Other Tales*, (Kestrel Books, 1974). © 1972 by Julius Lester. Reprinted by permission of Penguin Books Ltd.   ARNOLD LOBELL: 'The journey' from *Mouse Tales* (1972) and 'A list' from *Frog and Toad Together* (1973). Reprinted by permission of World's Work Ltd.   PAUL MILLS: 'Supposing . . .' Reprinted by permission of the author.   PHILIPPA PEARCE: *The great sharp scissors*, in the Listening and Reading Series (B.B.C. Publications, 1977). Reprinted by permission of the author. MICHAEL ROSEN: 'Mart was my best friend' first published in Teachers Notes for BBC Radio *That'd be Telling*. Reprinted by permission of the author.   ROBERT SCOTT: 'The doko' adapted from a retelling which appeared in *Folk Tales from Asia for Children Everywhere* (Book IV) prepared by the Asian Cultural Centre for UNESCO. Reprinted by permission of the author.   MARJORIE SHARMAT: Shortened version of *Nate the Great*. Reprinted by permission of World's Work Ltd.   MARY STOLZ: 'Me and the baby brother' from *Cricket & Company* Vol. 1, No. 8, (May 1975) published by the Open Court Publishing Company. Copyright © 1975 by Mary Stolz. Slightly adapted and reprinted by permission of the Roslyn Targ Literary Agency on behalf of the author.   SIV WIDERBERG: 'Nightmare' from *I'm Like Me* (1973), translated by Verne Moberg. Copyright 1968, 1969, 1970, 1971 by Siv Widerberg; trans. Copyright 1973 by Verne Moberg. Reprinted by permission of The Feminist Press.   ALISON CLAIRE WRIGHT: 'All by myself' first published in the *Daily Mirror* as a prize-winning entry to the 18th Daily Mirror Children's Literary Competition. Reprinted by permission of Mirror Group Newspapers Ltd.

All by myself

I'm standing around
In an empty room,
There's nobody here but me.
There's a stool in the corner,
There's a brick on the floor,
And, otherwise
There's only a door.

I'm sitting on the stool,
I'm standing on the brick,
I'm scampering on the floor,
And I've given the door a kick.

ALISON CLAIRE WRIGHT